SUMMARY & ANALYSIS

OF

—— MEDICAL MEDIUM ——

LIVER RESCUE

ANSWERS TO ECZEMA, PSORIASIS, DIABETES, STREP, ACNE,
GOUT, BLOATING, GALLSTONES, ADRENAL STRESS, FATIGUE,
FATTY LIVER, WEIGHT ISSUES, SIBO & AUTOIMMUNE DISEASE

A GUIDE TO THE BOOK
BY ANTHONY WILLIAM

BY **ZIP**READS

NOTE: This book is a summary and analysis and is meant as a companion to, not a replacement for, the original book.

Please follow this link to purchase a copy of the original book: https://amzn.to/2JGtRKt

TABLE OF CONTENTS

SYNOPSIS

Medical Medium Liver Rescue is a detailed manual to help solve the unknown problems that lurk in the livers of almost everyone on earth. Because we are not taught the importance of our livers or how to properly care for them, they become neglected, sluggish, and lead to a variety of diseases that modern medicine is unaware are related to poor liver function. Things such as menopausal hot flashes, high blood pressure and cholesterol, and digestive conditions such as IBS can all be traced back to poor liver function. Trendy fad diets that are high in fats and protein and low in carbs are only exacerbating the problem. Anthony William uses the power of the Spirit, who has spoken to him since he was a young boy, to uncover the true power of the liver, and he empowers you to give it the respect it deserves.

The book is divided into four sections, the first section focusing on the many functions of the liver, many of which science is still unaware of. William states that the liver performs more than 2,000 different functions, though he focuses only on the most important ones that are affecting your health.

In the second section, he addresses "sluggish liver" and how so many of us have been harming our livers without knowing it. He discusses the harmful effects of common diets and how little modern medicine truly knows about liver function. In the third section, he goes into far more detail about numerous diseases, their relation to liver function, and how viruses like EBV and bacteria such as strep play a part.

The fourth section is devoted to Liver Salvation and includes a wealth of resources on "troublemakers" that wreak havoc on our livers and modern diets that hurt more than they help. Finally, he presents in detail two diet plans to help reboot your liver function and clean out toxins as well as meal plans and recipes to accompany the diets.

PART I: WHAT DOES THE LIVER DO?

William opens the book with a call to recognize the true power of the liver. He argues that modern science understands very little about all that the liver does, but through his connection to the Spirit, he is able to see that the liver is truly a miraculous organ and an unsung hero of our physical and mental health.

Key Takeaway: The liver performs thousands of different functions, many currently unknown to modern science.

Many people are aware that the liver processes alcohol and cleanses toxins from our bodies, but it does much, much more than that. The liver processes fat and protects the pancreas. It's responsible for glucose, glycogen, vitamin, and mineral storage. It disarms and detains harmful materials; it screens and filters blood and provides you with its own immune function. The liver is a workhorse that is constantly struggling to maintain balance in your body while being bombarded by a toxic and unbalanced world.

Key Takeaway: The liver is the third brain of the body.

The liver is highly adaptable—even more so than the brain. If you think your liver mindlessly processes what you put into your body, you would be wrong. If you eat healthy during the week and then eat pizzas all weekend, your liver knows this and is ready for it. It produces additional bile in anticipation of highly fatty food consumption. The bile is necessary to break down the fats in the bloodstream, lest your blood become under-oxygenated. It's literally a survival mechanism.

Key Takeaway: Even healthy fats can lead to an overworked liver.

Whenever you eat fat, your liver releases bile to break it down and deliver the fat to your body as energy. The more fat you consume, the more bile the liver must produce. There are six levels of liver function based on the content and quality of fats in your diet:

Green – 15 percent or less fat in your diet, all from healthy sources like avocados, nuts, fish, and healthy oils like olive and coconut; normal bile production.

Yellow – 15 percent or less fat, but some of those fats are coming from unhealthy sources, causing the liver to increase bile production by 5 percent.

Orange – 15 to 30 percent dietary fat, but still from healthy sources. Bile levels rise up to 10 percent.

Orange-plus – 15 to 30 percent, but adding unproductive fats increases bile production by 15 to 20 percent.

Red – 30 to 40 percent fat, but all from healthy sources. Increased bile fluid and bile salts created to protect your longevity; the liver also releases calcium to protect the intestinal tract from the stronger, saltier "degreasing agent."

Red-plus – 30 percent or more dietary fat where some comes from fried foods, processed cooking oils, bacon grease, etc. The liver increases bile production up to 50 percent or more to stop the blood from thickening with fat intake.

Key Takeaway: Fat is the real culprit in insulin resistance.

The pancreas produces insulin. The liver does everything to stop excess fats from being processed in the pancreas because it leads to overproduction of insulin, and eventually to underproduction, or diabetes. The more fat in our bloodstreams and lymphatic systems, the more insulin we need to deliver glucose to those systems that run on it. Insulin resistance isn't caused by eating too many carbohydrates; the spike in blood sugar from eating too many carbohydrates is simply a *symptom* of insulin resistance from eating too much fat.

Key Takeaway: Sugar is crucial to liver function.

The liver stores glycose and glycogen to be released when your blood sugar drops in between meals. Without the liver, you would get that jittery, irritable, can't-concentrate feeling all the time. If you do get that feeling all the time, your liver is already struggling. The liver also *runs* on glucose, meaning that without sugars in your diet, the liver can't function at all. William reminds the reader that not all sugars are bad—focus on natural sugars from fruits, raw honey, squash, and potatoes. These sugars come bonded with nutrients that your body needs. If you don't feed your liver sugar, it will steal it from other parts of your body, which is why so many high-fat, high-protein diets are subtly introducing more sugars: you need them to function.

Key Takeaway: Your liver acts as a storage center and backup processor for nutrients.

When your body is running low on a specific nutrient, your liver turns to its backup storage to fill in the gap. When your stomach digests food, it sends the newly-converted minerals straight to the liver. The liver then goes through a miraculous process to protect those minerals. When it's time to send them to the organ that needs them, it creates a special, protective delivery system to send them safely where they need to go for maximum absorption. If your intestines are too damaged to convert the nutrients, the liver takes on the job. When your liver is too tired or damaged to act as a back-up, that is when you start seeing symptoms of digestive disorders like IBS.

Key Takeaway: We bombard the liver with toxins on a daily basis.

Synthetic pesticides and herbicides, pathogens, molds, plastics, and toxic heavy metals all carry an ionic charge that damages our bodily systems as they pass through. A healthy liver can discharge and neutralize that negative charge when toxins reach the liver. Beyond that, the liver can send out a chemical into the blood to disarm the toxins even before they arrive—a chemical undiscovered to modern medicine. If the liver can't discharge or disarm, however, it simply stores the toxins in what William describes as "trash heaps." Your body isn't meant to store these, but the liver does what it must. The deadliest toxins like DDT and petroleum get buried the deepest until the liver has time to process them properly.

Key Takeaway: Perime cells are undiscovered cells that aid in toxin storage.

The liver is not a static mass. While science is aware of lobules in the liver, these perime cells are produced by the lobules and can "shapeshift" to expand or contract toxin storage to prevent its release into the bloodstream. Perime cells cannot live outside of the liver, which is why they are undiscovered.

Key Takeaway: The liver is the ultimate processing plant.

William uses the metaphor of tiny elves watching a conveyor belt, sorting between the good and bad things as they enter your liver through your bloodstream. These elves are the lobules. If it can, your liver will "take out the trash" by sending toxins to be excreted through your colon as feces, through your kidneys as urine, or only in the worst case—loose in your bloodstream as free radicals. The elves want to package the toxins to keep them out of your bloodstream, but when your liver is overworked, undernourished, or already full of toxins, this process breaks down and can send the toxins to your heart and brain.

When too many toxins build up in the liver, the toxins get placed in hepatocyte cells, which eventually harden to stop the toxins from escaping, creating the scar tissue often found in liver diseases. As soon as we let our liver recover, it can "soften" those cells and process the toxins as it was designed to do in the first place. If we don't let the liver heal, however, and all of its primary lines of defense fail, it is forced to do what William calls hepatracking: using adrenaline to alert the elves and power them. This "alarm bell" William warns, is the last line of the liver's defense.

Key Takeaway: The liver has its own immune system of hepatic white blood cells.

These various types of white blood cells go out into the blood to stop viruses from attacking, monitor what enters the liver, and fight what tries to get in. These cells, which science has yet to discover, have highly specialized functions to protect the liver at all costs. William discusses each of their functions in detail.

PART II: DECODING THE LIVER

Key Takeaway: "Sluggish liver" is the result of years of neglect.

9 out of 10 people will experience sluggish liver in their lives, and it is the precursor to all other kinds of liver disease. Most of us take our livers for granted, never giving them the respect they deserve, which stops the liver from being able to do its job. We clean our houses from top to bottom, but fill our livers with trash. When our livers are overburdened, they can no longer filter and excrete the toxins; they must store them to be dealt with later. When we have too many toxins to store, the liver gets rid of nutrients to make room for all the trash it can't process. This is sluggish liver.

Key Takeaway: There are five types of sluggish liver each with unique symptoms.

Depending on which part of your liver is overburdened, you will experience different symptoms.

Middle – Hot flashes, swelling, low energy, weight gain, night sweats, irritability

Bottom – Insomnia, constipation, jealousy, emotional sensitivity

Top – Digestive issues, sores on the mouth, bulging belly

Left –Weakness on the left side of body, nausea, anxiousness, backaches

Right – Discolored nails, weakness on right side of the body, leg cramps, difficulty staying warm

Key Takeaway: Liver enzyme tests are still a guessing game for doctors.

Though William does believe liver enzyme tests can show *that* something is wrong with the liver, medical science still isn't sure exactly *what* elevated liver enzymes are telling us. Often, doctors will find elevated liver enzymes, test for a few other diseases, and send you home with a clean bill of health. The reality is that these enzymes are signaling other processes in your body to adapt to a situation your liver is dealing with. A sluggish liver may have accidentally released toxins into the blood and now the enzymes have to go find and destroy them. William notes that you can still have a serious liver condition even if your liver enzymes come back normal.

Key Takeaway: Chronic dehydration leads to dirty blood syndrome.

Most people are chronically dehydrated throughout their lives, which leads to a host of ailments. The liver counteracts this by storing living water molecules from fruit and vegetables to use when our bodies need it most, what William calls the "camel effect." The liver allows us to survive, but chronic dehydration leads to dirty blood as more toxins escape the liver's cleaning process. A sluggish liver and dirty blood can lead to a drop in stamina, dark under-eye circles, Raynaud's syndrome (discoloration of the skin, numbness in extremities), gout, varicose veins, inflammation, and insomnia,

Raynaud's syndrome in particular is caused by toxic viral waste from Epstein-Barr, is perfectly curable, and is not an auto-immune disorder. Gout is caused 100 percent by dirty blood. Many joint conditions are actually liver conditions. When gout patients experience "mystery edemas" around the joints, this is actually poor circulation due to a compromised liver.

The more chronically dehydrated you are, the dirtier and thicker your blood will become, the harder your body has to work to pump that blood, and the sicker you'll get.

Key Takeaway: Blood thickness determines how fatty your liver will become.

High blood fat is not currently measurable; your doctor can't tell you if you have it, but you probably do. Thick, fatty blood carries less oxygen, which starves the liver. One of the main misconceptions today is that fatty liver is caused by sugar intake. William points out that we usually eat sugar with fat or just after fat. The moment you consume fatty food, your liver starts producing bile to break down those fats and thin the blood. If you eat fatty foods your whole life, the liver weakens, and those fats seep out into your blood.

The liver, wanting to protect you, starts storing the fats itself, leading to fatty liver and to weight gain.

Key Takeaway: The liver is responsible for weight gain.

Despite popular opinion, no one has a "fast" or "slow" metabolism and the thyroid isn't responsible for weight gain. William explains that thyroid issues are usually viral, and viral infections weaken the liver, creating the connection between the two. The same is true for our adrenal glands, which have received a lot of attention lately as drivers of weight gain. The real connection is that stress causes excess adrenaline in our bodies, which the liver gets overworked trying to process and store. When the liver has to store things, weight gain usually follows.

Another reason the liver leads to weight gain is that strained livers sometimes pass off filtering to the lymphatic system, which leads to excess fluid retention. William closes the chapter with an impassioned plea to not judge the next obese person your see and to not judge yourself. Weight gain doesn't mean you're lazy, it just means your liver needs help.

Key Takeaway: Constant hunger is caused by deficiencies in the liver.

Your liver needs stores of glucose and glycogen to function. To make those compounds, it needs CCCs—Critical Clean Carbohydrates. When people are constantly, inexplicably hungry, it is their liver's way of trying to get them to eat the right kinds of carbohydrates. When pregnant women are constantly hungry it's because their liver is helping to develop the baby's liver. Hyper- and hypo-thyroidism are both caused by Epstein-Barr Virus, EBV, which usually starts off in the liver and eats up the glucose stores for itself, causing a shortage. This explains the connection between thyroidism and weight loss that doctors think is due to metabolic rates.

While the liver does need simple sugars to function, William stresses that sugars attached to fats don't help as the fat blocks the absorption of the sugars in the liver. It takes your body several hours to process different types of fat opening the door for glucose absorption. Animal fats take the longest to process, but healthier fats still take a few hours.

Key Takeaway: The liver is the key to anti-aging.

The only reason we age is because the liver is using its last resources to protect the most important parts of our bodies—the brain, the heart, and the pancreas—with all its might. This means less important organs, like the skin, suffer. When the liver receives antioxidants, it coats them in a special compound and sends them out into the body to prevent cell death. When the liver no longer receives these antioxidants in the diet, or does not have room to store them, it can no longer prevent that cell death and we start aging more rapidly.

PART III: SYMPTOMS AND CONDITIONS

DIABETES

While modern medicine believes that the pancreas is the source of diabetes, it is truly just a symptom of a liver problem. As one of the liver's main jobs is to protect the delicate pancreas, a sluggish liver can lead to toxins in the pancreas. As another one of the liver's main functions is to use its stored glucose and glycogen to maintain our blood sugar levels when we don't eat, as soon as those stores aren't fully stocked, the pancreas has to pick up the slack adjusting insulin levels to regulate blood sugar instead. Additionally, when the liver runs out of glucose and glycogen, it triggers adrenaline to make up for the shortfall of energy. This excessive adrenaline hurts the pancreas over time.

HIGH BLOOD PRESSURE

While many people are diagnosed with mystery hypertension, William argues the explanation is very simple: that same dirty, thick blood that is clogging up your liver is harder for the heart to pump, like sucking a milkshake through a straw compared to a glass of water. The increased workload on the heart leads to high blood pressure. Even those with a healthy diet who avoid alcohol can experience mystery hypertension due their livers being overstressed by toxins.

HIGH CHOLESTEROL

Doctors may tell you your diet is responsible for high cholesterol, and they're not totally wrong, but it ultimately starts in the liver. The liver is responsible for producing HDL, or good cholesterol, and managing LDL, bad cholesterol. A sluggish liver loses this ability. When your diet is filled with LDLs, the liver is too tired to produce HDLs and too busy to excrete the LDLs, so it stores as many as it can and releases the rest into your bloodstream. William argues that statin drugs meant to help cholesterol levels only mask the problem, and eventually make it worse.

HEART PALPITATIONS

Heart palpitations and arrythmias in an otherwise healthy heart are usually just chalked up to hormones or thyroid issues. This is because the medical community doesn't know what else to blame. William posits the culprits are actually the Epstein-Barr Virus (EBV) and buildups of DDT, pharmaceuticals, and petroleum byproducts in our livers.

These buildups in conjunction with EBV, over time, produce a jelly-like substance that the liver struggles to break down or contain. When the jelly breaks free from the liver, it creates miniscule buildups on the heart valves, causing mystery palpitations. With low blood–oxygen levels in dirty blood, the liver cannot break down this jelly.

ADRENAL PROBLEMS

Many trendy detox and cleanse diets are actually harming your liver more than helping. An intense detox can cause the adrenal glands to go into overdrive, releasing excess cortisol and adrenaline that your liver must also protect your body from by absorbing and neutralizing it. The liver does this by bonding the new hormones with old hormones it has stored up. This old-new pairing deactivates the potent adrenaline and makes it safe for release into the kidneys. But if your liver is sluggish or your adrenal glands are working overtime, those hormones can remain in your body for a long time, explaining why sometimes we can't let go of certain grievances attached to those old hormones.

CHEMICAL AND FOOD SENSITIVITIES

Many chemical and food sensitivities will seem to appear out of nowhere—where you once felt fine you are now overwhelmed with the synthetic perfumes in a department store or can no longer eat foods you once loved. As we know, the liver is responsible for processing the chemicals that enter your body and when it gets overwhelmed, it can no longer excrete them efficiently, causing a buildup. Some chemical sensitivity can also be related to EBV, or a combination of both. Luckily, there is hope. The right food can help cleanse your liver and lessen your adverse reactions or stop them entirely. William mentions both apples and lettuce as beneficial to the cause, which will be discussed in greater detail in the final section.

METHYLATION PROBLEMS

Methylation is the process by which your liver and ileum, working together, maximize the "bioavailability" of the nutrients your body receives for optimum function. If you received a diagnosis of an MTHRF gene mutation, fret not, your genes are not defective. This is just a marker that you're having methylation problems caused by a virus, most likely EBV.

B_{12} is the most important vitamin for liver function. And when the liver runs out because you don't eat enough salads, there is a wealth of B_{12} stored in the ileum. But if the ileum and liver are damaged, the B_{12} won't be methylated properly and it will hinder your organs' abilities to absorb other critical nutrients. Luckily, cleansing your liver can reverse much of this damaged functionality.

ECZEMA AND PSORIASIS

Many skin conditions are labeled as autoimmune—the body attacking itself—but William reiterates this is never the case. The body *never* attacks itself. Instead, all of these "mystery" skin conditions are due to the buildup of a particular toxin in the liver. Copper and mercury are two of the most common culprits. Combine the toxins with EBV and you get the most extreme skin conditions. EBV feeds on these toxins releasing an even more dangerous dermatoxin. Your body sends these toxins to your skin to get rid of them as a way to protect your internal organs. William presents detailed information on the specific toxins responsible for many different common and mystery skin conditions.

William notes that while steroids can be useful in treating the painful symptoms of some conditions, they are ultimately just masking the problem. The only real solution is changing your diet to allow your liver to clear out the toxins.

ACNE

Despite what most doctors think, acne is actually caused by a low-grade version of the *Streptococcus* bacteria. Strep feeds on antibiotics in the liver, which are commonly used to treat acne, and which stay in your liver from that ear infection you had as a baby or that chicken breast you ate. Acne usually hits at puberty because our immune systems weaken during puberty, allowing the strep to attack the lymphatic system. When the lymph nodes fight back, strep escapes through the skin. Remember that strep loves eggs, wheat, and dairy, so any of these foods can worsen acne.

SIBO

Small intestinal bacterial overgrowth is caused by a combination of an underproduction of bile leading to an underproduction of hydrochloric acid in the stomach and the liver's inability to separate some fats and proteins (due to poor diet) before entering the small intestine. These unprocessed fats then turn rancid, making delicious food for harmful bacteria. While the fungus *Candida* is often blamed for a rash of health problems, the truth is that we rely on it to help "take out the trash" in our bodies. When *Candida* isn't there to clean up the trash, the bad bacteria feed on it, causing SIBO, which is usually an overgrowth of *Streptococcus*. While the logical answer to a bacterial overgrowth is an antibiotic, William warns against this. Over the years, strep has evolved to be incredibly resistant to most antibiotics and even feeds on them. So using antibiotics to treat SIBO is instead feeding it. Instead, William recommends celery juice as being extremely restorative to the gut, strengthening your hydrochloric acids and white blood cells and increasing their power to fight the strep.

BLOATING, CONSTIPATION, AND IBS

When the liver becomes sluggish, the bile it produces to help break down foods weakens. Adrenaline production is another cause of poor bile production. As mentioned, poor bile production leads to poor hydrochloric acid production, both of which lead to fats and proteins entering the intestinal tract without being fully digested first. This feeds pathogens like strep, staph, and *E. Coli* causing bloating, intestinal and colonic inflammation, and constipation. Consuming a lot of wheat, dairy, and eggs can intensify the situation leading to irritable bowel syndrome. While these may seem like stomach problems, the weakened liver is at the root of them all.

BRAIN FOG

Despite what medical science would have you believe, brain fog is not related to gut health. It is related directly to neurotoxins (often byproducts of EBV) escaping from your liver into your bloodstream and crossing the blood-brain barrier. These neurotoxins can also be released by adrenalin overproduction caused by prolonged stress or by a buildup of heavy metals. As we know, all of these things weaken the liver. William wants you to know that you shouldn't feel lazy, stupid, or inadequate because you suffer from confusion or exhaustion. Brain fog isn't your fault, and it can be cured.

EMOTIONAL LIVER: MOOD STRUGGLES AND SAD

Seasonal Affective Disorder, SAD, is a recently new condition to describe the physical and emotional changes many people experience as the seasons change from warm and sunny to cold and cloudy. But William argues this is not the case. The seasons may be a trigger for some, but they are most likely exacerbating a condition that already exists, and therefore, will continue to worsen each passing year. Anxiety, depression, aches and pains, sadness, can all be explained by the effect your liver is having on your brain.

Mercury in the blood causes focus and concentration to drop. Frustration and anger can arise from a fatty or pre-fatty liver. The liver itself has its own emotions which can be transferred to us—just look at recipients of liver transplants who take on the emotions of their donors. The emotions that trigger a surge of adrenaline, like a heartbreak, are also kept in the liver when it stores that adrenaline. When it finally releases it, you will feel those emotions again. The liver goes through these emotional purges often on a seasonal basis, hence the connection to SAD. More importantly, however, our diets change in winter, consuming more unhealthy fats with the holiday season, which further triggers these effects.

PANDAS, JAUNDICE, AND BABY LIVER

We are born with livers already contaminated by the livers of our parents and grandparents, working at only 70 percent of what they should be. Acid reflux in babies is caused by what William calls baby liver—a baby born with a liver already struggling to make the little bile it needs to digest breast milk. Jaundice in babies is the same exact thing, though doctors believe it's that the baby's liver hasn't developed enough yet. This is wrong. It's the liver already fighting to cleanse itself of toxins. This can continue into childhood causing many physical symptoms and emotional outbursts as well.

Pediatric Autoimmune Neuropsychiatric Disorders Associated with Streptococcal infections, PANDAS, is a theoretical disorder that leads to autoimmune responses as well as tics, spasms, and OCD. William argues these neurological symptoms are actually from a viral infection (usually HHV-6) triggered by high mercury levels, and that strep is simply a cofactor of a weakened immune system.

AUTOIMMUNE LIVER AND HEPATITIS

If someone has an inflamed liver, the first thing doctors will turn to is Hepatitis. They will decide which type of hepatitis you have based on some grouping of symptoms, not on a confirmable difference in types. All types of hepatitis are actually the same virus and they don't have a definitive way of testing for it yet. That's why one patient can get a hepatitis C diagnosis while another patient with similar symptoms can get a Cirrhosis diagnosis. William argues that hepatitis isn't even its own virus, its many variations are all caused by different mutated strains of Epstein-Barr.

William also argues that basically every autoimmune disorder you can think of actually originates as a viral infection in your liver. He repeats: your body will never attack itself.

CIRRHOSIS AND LIVER SCAR TISSUE

Pericirrhosis is a state of pre-pre-cirrhosis that many people are afflicted by, yet they have no idea. While alcohol abuse can lead to cirrhosis and damage your liver, William reminds the reader not to judge—anyone can be affected by pericirrhosis. Cirrhosis is simply scar tissue accumulating on the liver faster than it can rejuvenate itself. This only happens when the liver is so full of toxins it can't keep up. Luckily, cirrhosis can be stopped in its tracks and even reversed. Scar tissue can be softened with the right antiviral foods and antioxidants.

LIVER CANCER

The way cancer forms in the liver is by interacting with a particular virus. Not all strains of EBV can cause cancer, but some can, along with strains of shingles, and many herpetic viruses. For these viruses to cause cancer, they still need lots of food in the liver, like chemicals, heavy metals, and proteins from eggs and dairy. If you eat lettuce and apples and healthy fruits and vegetables, however, the viruses will get weaker. The viruses feed on those troublemakers that are stored in your liver, creating an even-more-toxic environment that eventually kills the viral cells, mutating them into cancer cells. Only by starving the cancer cells of the toxic food they love can you stop its progress.

GALLBLADDER SICKNESS

The gallbladder is a tiny organ tucked beneath the right side of your liver that stores its bile. Also in the gallbladder is a kind of "sludge" that doctors dismiss as normal and harmless. But the truth is that sludge is a trail of your toxic exposures from your entire life. Doctors don't want to look at the gallbladder because the capitalist industrial machine would collapse if we knew how much they had been poisoning us all these years.

When you get food poisoning, the gallbladder can also store that virus, along with strep, for many years to come causing infections that doctors don't understand. Most types of gallstones are also caused by an overstressed liver. When a liver works too hard and overheats, certain poisons can end up "fusing" together with dead red blood cells and then cooling and turning into stones when they reach the gallbladder. Many gallbladder issues are connected to issues with the liver overheating and the body having to work even harder to cool the gallbladder.

PART IV: LIVER SALVATION

William begins the final section of the book with an ode to the power of the liver as our great protector, like a mother who protects her child. The liver will sacrifice anything to keep us healthy, and we must return the favor by treating our livers with the respect and admiration they deserve.

Key Takeaway: The liver works on a 3:6:9 cycle.

According to William, the liver will fully regenerate its cells every nine years, like clockwork. This happens in thirds, usually three months before each three-year mark. William notes, however, that if you're not allowing your liver to cleanse, it can still be reborn with the same toxins and pathogens infecting it as before. This is why it's incredibly important to treat your liver with kindness just before any birthday that is a multiple of three.

Key Takeaway: Many common liver remedies do more damage than good.

Consuming ox bile is an accepted remedy to low bile production in humans, but William argues this is like allowing a foreign invader to attack your body. It confuses your liver and won't help bile production in any way. If you have problems with bile production, celery juice is the best remedy.

Eating liver is an ancient—and incorrect—medical theory on improving liver function. Of course, as we now know how many toxins are stored in the livers of both humans and animals, consuming those toxins will only further stress our own livers. Not to mention, the precious enzymes and minerals in an animal's liver aren't the same ones we need as humans.

While apples are one of the most beneficial fruits for our livers, apple cider vinegar is not the cure-all it's made out to be. William admits that if you must consume vinegar, ACV is the best one, but any vinegar is damaging to the liver the same way any alcohol is. A little ACV on a salad is fine, but avoid using it daily or as part of a liver flush.

Coffee enemas have no benefit for the liver, and the increased adrenaline triggered by the caffeine is actually damaging to the liver. Alkaline water is touted as beneficial, but when our stomachs have to neutralize the pH of something coming in, they are distracted from their other jobs and often the liver has to step in to help.

Most importantly, William warns against any liver cleanses or flushes that utilize oil. Drinking olive oil is NOT a solution and will only make your liver work harder to produce more bile to break it down. The "lumps" you may pass during the cleanse are not liver stones or gallbladder stones, they are just clumps of oil coagulated with debris from your gut.

Key Takeaway: Fruits are not the enemy.

Many new fad diets tout fruit and fructose as the enemy, claiming fructose intolerance is making you sick and recommending more fats instead. Of course, this is wrong. The reason your body isn't absorbing the fructose properly is because it's overwhelmed with all of the fats it has to digest. When it can't keep up, you get rancid fats in your intestines and you get even more sick. Get rid of the fats, keep eating the fruits, and see what happens. Similarly, lectin has recently become a scapegoat for health problems. William insists this is ridiculous, lectins do not harm us.

Key Takeaway: Diet science has gotten it all wrong.

William recounts how we got to this current idea that high-protein, low-carb diets are the best answer for longevity. Science was right to start removing many added fats and sugars and processed foods, but animal protein is higher in fat than anyone realizes. And high-fat diets are the worst for our livers. Our bodies need sugars, and removing the natural, healthy sugars from fruits and starchy vegetables has caused more harm than people realize. Allowing berries and avocados and apples to enter these trendy, high-fat, low-carb, low-sugar diets happened because science inadvertently realized that humans can't survive without these natural sugars. In fact, your liver loves these natural sugars. The sugars that come attached to fruit and veggies are especially easy for your liver to process to take the glucose and glycogen it needs.

William does concede that high-fat, low-carb diets focused on reducing junky, processed foods, and consuming more vegetables can help compared to a diet of fast food and daily sodas, but ultimately those fats will still build up in your liver.

The radical fats in our diets—fats that we eat with proteins and sugars, such as cheese on a ham sandwich with mayo or butter on a corn cob—should ideally be separated. William recommends snacking on leafy greens or cucumbers about 20 minutes before you consume a meal with radical fats.

Key Takeaway: Fruits are the missing piece of the puzzle.

No matter if you are vegan, paleo, or vegetarian, your diet is high in animal fats or vegetable fats, you are most likely consuming too much fat and not enough fruit. Most trendy diets today decided to lump fruits in with all the bad sugars and carbohydrates out there. Fruit sugars, however, are vastly different and are processed by your body in much different ways. The sugars in fruit allow your body to absorb nutrients you otherwise couldn't. This is one of the hidden powers of fruits.

TROUBLEMAKERS

The perimeter surface, the subsurface, and the deep inner core are the three depths of the liver for storing different troublemakers. You can think of these like the skin, flesh, and core of an apple. The deeper a troublemaker is stored in your liver, the longer it will take to cleanse. William provides an extensive list of the troublemakers you should work at all costs to avoid, as well as guidelines on how long they will take to cleanse and where in the liver they tend to collect. He admits it isn't always possible to completely avoid them. Just do your best.

PETROCHEMICALS

Plastics, gasoline and diesel, engine oil and grease, exhaust fumes, kerosene, lighter fluid, gas grills and ovens, chemical solvents, dioxins, lacquer, paint, paint thinner, and carpet chemicals.

All of these toxins enter our liver from everyday activities like pumping gas, cooking dinner on the stove, painting your house, or cleaning the kitchen. They reside in various layers of the liver and can take a long time to cleanse.

CHEMICAL NEUROANTAGONISTS

Chemical fertilizers, insecticides and pesticides, DDT, fungicides, smoke exposure, fluoride, and chlorine.

This group is highly toxic, enters all three levels of the liver, and takes the longest for the liver to remove. DDT is mentioned separately as it has an extremely long shelf life and will continue to persist in the livers of your children and their children if not removed.

PROBLEMATIC FOOD CHEMICALS

Aspartame and other artificial sweeteners, MSG, formaldehyde, other preservatives.

Most basic food preservatives stay at the surface of the liver, but can be found even in foods that claim to be preservative free. Aspartame, MSG, and formaldehyde, however, go straight to the deep, inner core and are far more nefarious.

PROBLEMATIC FOODS

Eggs, dairy, cheese, food hormones, high-fat foods, recreational alcohol, excessive vinegar, caffeine, excessive salt, gluten, corn, canola oil, pork products.

Eggs, dairy, gluten, corn, and cheese are some of the favorite foods of pathogens. Vinegar is almost as bad as alcohol at inhibiting liver function. Salt is ok in moderation, but should be natural, not added, and not in combination with radical fats. Canola oil contains harsh chemical compounds. Pork products are extremely high in fat.

PATHOGENS

Viruses and viral waste matter (including EBV shingles, and herpetic viruses), bacteria (including strep, staph, and E. Coli), food-borne toxins, mold.

William stresses the way to fight these pathogens is to remove their food sources. The time to remove them from the liver will vary with your ability to remove other toxins and buildup that can also function as food sources.

CHEMICAL INDUSTRY DOMESTIC INVASION

Plug-in air fresheners, scented candles, aerosol air-fresheners, spray-bottle air fresheners, cologne and aftershave, perfumes and scented lotions and creams, hairspray, hair dye, talcum powder, conventional makeup, spray tan, nail chemicals, conventional household cleaners, laundry detergent, dry-cleaning chemicals.

This group is likely the hardest to avoid completely as you will always be subject to someone's perfume on the train or the cleaning supplies in a public bathroom. Scented air-fresheners are everywhere. Many conventional makeup items are full of heavy metals and hair dye chemicals are a favorite food of EBV. You won't be able to avoid these entirely, but remove as many from your home as you can and opt for organic versions whenever possible.

PHARMACEUTICALS

Antibiotics, antidepressants, anti-inflammatories, sleeping pills, biologics, immunosuppressants, amphetamines, opioids, statins, blood pressure medication, hormone medications, thyroid medications, steroids, birth control, alcohol, recreational drugs.

William doesn't insist that you stop taking all medications that could be helping you deal with various diseases or ailments. Just be aware and question before you start taking any new drugs. Alcohol isn't just recreational, but also exists in a variety of toiletries and over-the-counter medications.

TOXIC HEAVY METALS

Mercury, lead, aluminum, copper, cadmium, barium, nickel, arsenic.

Heavy metals can enter our systems through city water, restaurant food, pots and pans, insecticides, pharmaceuticals, or even jet fuel falling from the sky. They take a long time to remove completely from the liver and can be passed through many generations.

RADIATION

Airplanes, x-rays, MRIs, cell phones, and irradiated food all leak radiation into our bodies. Even standing next to someone who got an x-ray can affect you. Radiation can take several years to cleanse completely, and William recommends a heavy metal smoothie to aid the process.

EXCESS ADRENALINE

Prolonged adrenal stress and adrenaline-based activities can flood the liver with adrenaline as it tries to shield the body from its harmful effects. Adrenaline is also a fuel for EBV and other viruses. William doesn't recommend avoiding sex or rollercoasters, just take care of your liver so you're not overloading it.

RAINFALL EXPOSURE

Sadly, our rainfall is now filled with chemicals being spewed by industrial factories around the world. Rogue byproducts fill the atmosphere and get absorbed into our skin when it rains. Luckily, rain itself is living water that aids the liver in its removal of the toxins it contains.

HEALING FOODS, HERBS & SUPPLEMENTS

Key Takeaway: The liver needs oxygen, water, sugar, then mineral salts, in that order.

William recommends that whatever your current diet is, try to cut back at least 25 percent of the fats you're eating. Replace a handful of nuts with a handful of berries, or cut back from one avocado to just half of one per day. Take as many sources of fat as possible and replace them with an item from the list of liver-healing foods. For each food, William provides a brief explanation of its healing power—both how it works to heal the liver and what conditions it is most beneficial for treating. For a full guide, please purchase a copy of the original book.

Key Takeaway: The healing foods for your liver.

Foods listed in bold are mentioned as particular champions of strong liver health, liver nutrition, or cleansing properties. Foods marked with a ★ are particularly important to liver health.

Apples★ – Apples are your liver's best friend. Eat them often.

Apricots – Medicine for your liver, anti-aging

Artichokes – Stop growth of tumors and cysts

Arugula – Gentle purging effect

Asparagus★ – Calming and cleansing for the liver, one of the most potent liver-healing foods

Atlantic Sea Vegetables – Antiseptic to bacteria, strengthen bile salts

Bananas★ – The liver's favorite source of food; improve ability to absorb nutrients

Berries – "A medicine chest for the liver;" protect from troublemakers

Broccoli – Helps liver's immune function; be sure to eat the stalks

Brussels sprouts – Extreme liver cleansing, helps escort toxins out of the liver

Carrots – Quick way to refuel your liver

Celery★ – Restores bile production and hydrochloric acid balance

Cherries – Helps bind to toxins to cleanse

Cilantro – Helps remove heavy metals

Coconut –Can help lower viral loads, use only in moderation

Cranberries – Prevent toxic overload, help break free troublemakers

Cruciferous Vegetables – Help replenish your nutrient storage banks

Cucumbers – Living water hydration for the liver; anti-inflammatory

Dandelion greens – Potent liver-cleanser

Dates – Eliminate mucus from intestinal tract; fuel source

Eggplant – Improves blood flow to liver; thins out dirty blood

Figs – Easy to digest, bind to poisons along the way

Garlic – "A pathogen's worst nightmare"

Grapes – Longevity food; help dissolve gallstones

Hot peppers – Increases blood flow; resets the liver

Sunchokes – Protect from fast-spreading illness

Kale – Starves bad bacteria; improves B_{12} production

Kiwis – Powerful gallstone dissolver

Leafy greens – Full of liver-friendly micronutrients

Lemons and limes – Hydrochloric acid and bile production

Mangoes – Help to cool a toxic, overworked liver

Maple Syrup – An "IV for the liver"

Melons – Liver hydration; thin out toxic, fat-filled blood

Mushrooms – Antifungal, detoxifying

Onions and scallions – Antimicrobial; cooling properties

Oranges and tangerines - Helps nutrient absorption

Papayas   -   Sooth   intestinal   tract;   reduce inflammation

Parsley – Dislodges poisons; helps clean gallbladder sludge

Peaches and Nectarines – Help to cleanse intestines

Pears – Calming fruit good for overburdened livers

Pineapple – Dissolves gallstones

Dragon fruit★ – Helps cell regeneration in the liver

Pomegranates – Cleanse blood vessels, improving flow

Potatoes★ – Help build up glycogen storage; fight fatty liver

Radishes – Liver disinfectant; help white blood cells

Raw honey – Antimicrobial, antiviral, antifungal, antibacterial

Red cabbage – Minimizes pathogens in intestinal tract

Spinach – Nutrient powerhouse; aids all liver function

Sprouts and Microgreens★ – Elevated biotics to create beneficial bacterial environment

Sweet potatoes – Glucose and glycogen food storage for liver

Tomatoes – Nutrient-rich; aid all liver health and function

Turmeric (fresh) – Purges troublemakers; protects liver cells

Wild blueberries★ – Undiscovered antioxidants; antiaging

Winter squash – Important nutrients for liver storage

Zucchini – Liver hydration; purging effect; reduce gallbladder inflammation

Key Takeaway: Healing herbs and supplements for general liver health.

William notes that not everyone needs to deal with herbs and supplements—just focusing on foods is OK too. If you choose to experiment with supplements, make sure any tinctures are alcohol- and ethanol-free and avoid supplements with dozens of various ingredients. Each of these supplements should be taken individually. Below is a list of supplements that are beneficial to anyone, however the original book contains a guide to which supplements are best depending on what you may be suffering from. If you are suffering from multiple ailments, William recommends you focus on the one causing you the most discomfort and distress.

5-MTHF (5-methyltetrahydrofolate):	ALA (alpha lipoic acid)
Aloe vera	Amla berry
Ashwagandha	Barley grass juice powder
B-complex	Black walnut
Burdock root	Cardamom
Cat's Claw	Chaga mushroom
Chicory root	Coenzyme Q10
Curcumin	Dandelion root
D-mannose	EPA and DHA
Eyebright	Ginger
Glutathione	Goldenseal
Hibiscus	Lemon balm
Licorice root	L-lysine
Magnesium glycinate	Melatonin
Milk thistle	MSM
Mullein Leaf	NAC (N-acetyl cysteine)
Nascent iodine	Nettle leaf
Olive leaf	Oregon grape root
Peppermint	Raspberry leaf
Red clover	Rose hips
Schisandra berry	Selenium
Spirulina	Turmeric
Vitamin B_{12}	Vitamin C
Vitamin D_3	Wild blueberry powder
Yellow dock	Zinc

LIVER RESCUE MORNING

You and your liver go to bed at the same time, but your liver gets up around three or four in the morning to get back to work. When you wake up, immediately hydrate with lemon water, celery juice, or cucumber juice to help flush out the waste the liver was busy packaging overnight. Until you feed it radical fats, your liver can keep detoxing all morning long.

- A squeeze of lime juice or a few slices of cucumber activate your water, making it more beneficial

- You can eat before lunchtime, but avoid any type of radical fat

- Focus on hydrating and flushing fruits and vegetables in the morning like apples, papayas, grapes, and tangerines.

- "Healthy" high-protein foods like nuts, egg whites, or turkey bacon are still high in fat and will stop the detox process

- Eat every one-to-two hours to maintain blood sugar and take pressure off the liver

- Avoid caffeine if possible

LIVER RESCUE 3:6:9

If Liver Rescue Morning is meant to be an everyday, easy-to-do improvement to your liver, Liver Rescue 3:6:9 is a more intensive program to dig deeper. It is a nine-day program in three, three-day intervals. The numbers are not random, the liver functions in multiples of threes with lobules being six-sided and a new stream of blood flushing the liver every nine heartbeats, among many others. William recommends the average person do the 3:6:9 program every two to three months, but you can do it more frequently if you feel plagued by troublemakers.

This is merely an overview of the program. For the full guidelines of Liver Rescue 3:6:9, you will need to purchase a copy of the original book.

For the first three days, you will follow Liver Rescue Morning with 16 ounces of lemon or lime water. You will have three meals each day as well as snacks in between meals to keep up your blood sugar, all within the guidelines. This is meant to ease you into liver detox, do not skip this part.

- No gluten, dairy, eggs, lamb, pork, canola oil

- No fats before dinner, reduce by 50 percent overall

- One animal product per day allowed, only at dinner

- Two apples with 1-4 dates every afternoon, increasing each day

The guidelines for the "The 6" remain the same as for "The 3" except you are no longer allowed an animal product with dinner. Celery juice is a key component of the 6 as it has numerous benefits for the liver. Remember that celery juice is a tonic, not a meal, and you will need to eat food about 20 minutes afterward. William provides very specific timing and recipes for the 6 that you will need to purchase in order to properly partake in the 3:6:9, but general guidelines are provided below.

- 16 ounces of lemon or lime juice + 16 ounces celery juice

- NO radical fats or animal products allowed

- Lots of asparagus and brussels sprouts

- 2-3 apples per day

- Eat as much as you want of approved foods

In your final three days you will be giving your liver everything it needs to work hard and cleanse itself. Don't starve yourself—your liver needs the fuel more than ever. Stick to the guidelines from the 6 plus follow the recommend recipes. Day 9 will be a liquid diet to assist in the flushing of toxins.

- Increased celery juice

- At least 2-3 apples per day

- Liquid-heavy recipes to assist cleansing

- Squash, potatoes, asparagus, brussels sprouts

William recommends that you ease out of the cleanse, not jumping immediately to a bacon and egg breakfast on day 10.

Chapter 39 is devoted entirely to different recipes including juices, teas, and broths, liver rescue smoothies and salads, and even desserts such as bananas foster and peach ginger sorbet. William stresses that when you are eating liver-healthy foods, there is no need for moderation. You can eat as much as you want since those foods aren't stressing out your liver.

Key Takeaway: There are several meditations that can help liver healing.

William provides detailed instructions on how to engage in a series of mediations to help aid in your liver health. These include the Peaceful Liver Bath, Liver Cooling, Liver Regeneration, a mediation to strengthen bile production and one to help destroy viruses and other pathogens. There is a morning meditation to strengthen your liver's immune function, and another to loosen fat cells in the liver. He offers a nighttime meditation to reverse disease and one to help eliminate toxins—the core goal of the entire book.

KEY TAKEAWAY: THE STORM WILL PASS.

William closes the book with a rumination on self-love, passion, compassion, free will, and peace. He urges you to find compassion not only for others, but for yourself. Love yourself unconditionally. No matter what you think, no matter what you're struggling with, you have not done this to yourself. Even if you made choices that ultimately hurt your liver, you didn't know any better—the world has not told us how important the liver truly is or how to care for it. We focus too often on the world around us and forget to care for the world inside of ourselves. If you are suffering from disease or loss or heartbreak, know that these things will pass because everything changes. Sometimes it may change for the worse, but know that it will always change again. And know that only by living a life of peace—peace with yourself and peace with others and peace with those things you can't control—can you become a beacon to those around you.

EDITORIAL REVIEW

Medical Medium Liver Rescue is William's fourth book and the first to be devoted solely to liver function. While his previous books focused on the thyroid, Epstein-Barr Virus, and life-changing foods, all of the previous works are closely tied to the healthy functioning of the liver. The reader will be surprised to learn just how many ailments and conditions can be linked back to a sluggish liver, many of which doctors have no idea about.

William's writing is easily accessible, though scientific at times. For every scientific, biological explanation, however, he provides rich, visual metaphors to help the reader understand the processes their bodies are going through with every daily attack on the liver. As with all of his books, the writing maintains a degree of spirituality. He begs the reader to understand the true spiritual power of the liver as not only a healer, but as an emotional center of the human body. Your liver isn't only removing physical toxins from your blood, but emotional ones as well. The liver is as important as the heart and the brain, and yet modern medicine has mostly overlooked it. William does not provide any sources or cite any relevant studies in his books, as his knowledge comes directly from the Spirit.

His guides to the foods and toxins to be welcomed and avoided are detailed with helpful explanations on the particular benefits of each and every one. While those benefits are covered briefly here, it is recommended to purchase the original book in order to fully grasp the power of the foods and supplements he recommends. In addition, the two diets he presents—the Morning Liver Rescue and Liver Rescue 3:6:9—are both easy to follow and come with any recipes, guides, and substitutions one may need. Again, these cannot be fully divulged in a summary, and the reader is encouraged to purchase the original book before embarking on any dietary changes.

Whether or not you partake in his specific diets, however, the book is a trove of information on how anyone can improve their liver function and reverse disease. Even if you are skeptical of William's connection to the Spirit, his detailed understanding of the internal workings of the human body may have you second-guessing your faith in modern medicine.

Overall, the book is a valuable resource and worthwhile read for anyone who has been suffering from mystery illnesses and dealing with medications that never seem to provide a cure. Even if you aren't suffering yet, his book can help you improve your mood, your energy, and prevent ailments that may have been lurking in a liver that's overworked and unable to handle the myriad toxins we're exposed to every day. A healthier liver is the ultimate de-stressor; it is the key to fighting aging and a wealth of other disorders. William's book will show you the way to empower your liver—and the rest of your body—to help you become your best self.

BACKGROUND ON AUTHOR

Anthony William is a *New York Times* bestselling author. He was born with a unique gift of communicating with a higher power, the Spirit. When he was four years old, he shocked his family by declaring his symptom-free grandmother had lung cancer. Medical testing soon confirmed his diagnosis.

He uses his gift to unravel many of the mysteries of modern life, in particular, health-related mysteries. Over the years, his insight has become invaluable to doctors and prominent personalities who attest to its accuracy and reliability.

Williams has authored numerous books including *Medical Medium: Secrets Behind Chronic and Mystery Illness and How to Finally Heal* and *Medical Medium: Thyroid Healing.*

TITLES BY ANTHONY WILLIAM

Medical Medium: Secrets Behind Chronic and Mystery Illness and How to Finally Heal (2015)

Medical Medium: Life-Changing Foods (2016)

Medical Medium: Thyroid Healing (2017)

Medical Medium: Liver Rescue (2018)

If you enjoyed this *ZIP Reads* publication, we encourage you to purchase a copy of <u>the original book.</u>

We'd also love an honest review on Amazon.com!

ZIPREADS

39512107R00034

Made in the USA
Lexington, KY
19 May 2019